Here Con
The Eden

Celebrating 90 years of Eden Bus Services

Stuart Gray

ISBN 9781905304820

Contents

(Front Cover)
CPT 800 is a Bedford WTB with Duple bodywork. The location is unknown but the photo was taken by George Summerson who pursued a keen hobby in photography and took many photos of life at the family business, and developed the photos at his own dark room in his house. *(Summerson Family Collection)*

(Back Cover)
Leyland Tiger HD 7846 heels over as it completes the left turn from Spennymoor towards Middlestone Moor en route to West Auckland, with an OK passing behind heading towards Bishop Auckland at the area known as the Four Lane Ends. *(Stuart Bell Collection)*

(Title Page)
8111 UP, a Bedford SB5 with Duple Bella Vista bodywork, seen when new at the Eden Garage. This coach was usually found on contract work but also on the service from Shildon to Stockton which operated twice a week and provided a touch of comfort to the many housewives of Shildon and Newton Aycliffe who visited the huge and popular market. *(Summerson Family Collection)*

FOREWORD

The Eden. Mention that name to anyone above a certain age in Bishop Auckland, and thoughts turn to immaculately presented red and ivory buses, crewed by cheery staff operating a reliable and punctual bus service, in all weathers. Indeed, it is often said, "The Eden always got through!"

To the general enthusiast fraternity, I have felt that The Eden always lived in the shadow of its more famous neighbours, OK Motor Services and United Automobile, and precious little is known except to those that had a passionate interest in the company.

I was brought up with The Eden service. I grew up in Kirk Merrington and our family did not possess a car, therefore all our travelling was done by bus and usually by The Eden, for trips into Spennymoor for shopping and to visit my Grandmother. A strong interest in buses was nurtured from an early age but really began one day when waiting for the bus with my mother, The Eden duly arrived but rather than a usual Leyland Leopard service bus, it was a huge coach, with trapezoid windows and massive EDEN logos on the side, standing proudly in gold. They towered above my infant head and I was utterly spellbound, to the point that mother had to forcibly drag me on this coach!

Later in life I got to know one of the great Eden characters by the name of Steve Foster, who gave me the inspiration to commence this work. Steve was, and is, passionate about all things Eden and began a sizeable collection of photographs, records and anecdotes which he passed to me.

Though The Eden was sold to North East Bus (the parent company of United) in 1995, and the name faded away under the corporate image of Arriva, the name 'The Eden' was rescued by Graeme Scarlett, a Shildon businessman who drove for The Eden in the 1970s. It was a bit of a 'Victor Kiam' moment, he liked the company so much, he bought it. Consequently, Eden buses still ply the streets of Bishop Auckland as though nothing happened, and even (at the time of writing) running out of the garage established in West Auckland, by the Summerson Brothers in the 1930s.

The object of this book is to celebrate the history of this plucky little independent bus operator, and to bring to the attention of bus enthusiasts everywhere the fortunes of The Eden. With that in mind, this book is dedicated to the staff, past and present, of The Eden who provided a reliable and friendly service to the people of South West Durham.

I would also like to offer my grateful thanks to everyone who has assisted me in compiling this book, there are too many to list but special thanks must go the aforementioned Steve Foster, whose infectious enthusiasm led me to this lengthy project, to John Godfrey, the former traffic manager of The Eden who passed on much information. The Kithead Trust in Droitwich was also the source of some valuable information and I thank their detailed and speedy response to a query I had. The Summerson family have also provided much information, support and photographs and I am forever indebted to their assistance.

Final special thanks must go to the current custodian of The Eden, Graeme Scarlett, who allows me an 'open house' policy at The Eden garage, and frequent visits have been made when in need of motivation and inspiration. Graeme also kindly contributed his words to the last chapter of this book detailing his work in re-establishing the company.

Stuart Gray

The coach that began my lifelong fascination with The Eden is the striking V1 (LTN 753X), a Volvo B58 with Duple Dominant 3 bodywork. When new, V1 would be used on tour work in the United Kingdom and Europe, but to satisfy the terms of the new bus grant under which it was purchased, would also find use on local service work. The striking bodywork caused many heads to turn as it passed, this design of coach was not common in South West Durham! *(Summerson Family Collection)*

959 CPT was a Leyland Tiger Cub with unusual Duple Midland bodywork. Numbered C5 (or 'Cub 5'), it was delivered in the very smart original Eden livery. C5 was a regular on the Bishop Auckland-Aycliffe service and served the company for over 10 years. The picture is taken in the grounds of the Eden Garage when new in 1959. *(Summerson Family Collection)*

1 – EARLY DAYS OF THE EDEN

In 1927 'The Eden Bus Service' commenced by George Summerson, a resident of West Auckland, which is a village located some four miles from Bishop Auckland. At the time, 'Bishop' which it was and still is colloquially referred to, was a thriving market town surrounded by the colliery industry. The two Aucklands had been served by a plethora of bus operators and it was good bus operating territory, the main road for the most part bisected heavily populated areas. Further west from West Auckland was the village of Evenwood, home to Wade Emmerson who established the well known OK Motor Services, but known initially as Gaunless Valley Motor Services.

Bus services between Bishop Auckland and Evenwood were hotly contested by several bus operators, including OK, and also the United Automobile company, in a time when licensing for bus service operation was not as tightly regulated as one might expect – basically, a man could buy a bus, apply to the local authority for a licence to run on a set route on a timetable, and off he went.

However in practice, the timetables weren't worth the paper they were written on and buses of competing concerns would battle to get the most passengers on at any time. There are stories of opposing crews literally fighting in the streets and racing each other to bus stops. One operator even offered a free 'dip' to late night passengers coming out of the cinemas. (A dip is a Bishop Auckland delicacy consisting of a bread bun dipped in pork fat – it does taste better than it sounds!)

This situation had been going on for at least fifteen years when George decided to set up his operation. He had been trained by and worked for United Automobile and also for Wade Emmerson as a motor mechanic, both at Bishop Auckland. George also successfully passed the required examinations to acquire membership of the Institute of the Motor Industry (IMI) and became a fully qualified mechanical engineer.

No doubt George had seen the potential to operate his own omnibus service and business with his experience at United and OK, and especially one from his home town of West Auckland. He

The first two buses purchased by George Summerson were Chevrolets, seating only 14 but probably started out life as a lorries. Here one is posed with a youthful looking conductor, who is believed to be George Lowes, who worked for the Summersons from a young age and dedicated much of his working life on The Eden. *(Summerson Family Collection)*

As the business grew, heavier and more rugged buses were desired to cope with the rough road conditions. Leyland chassis were favoured and MS 9194, a Leyland LT1 acquired second hand, is pictured here, once again posed with staff. *(Summerson Family Collection)*

Hutchinsons were another small operator based in West Auckland who for a short while operated the West Auckland-Spennymoor route with Summerson Brothers. They also appear to have been involved with the West Auckland-Bishop Auckland corridor judging by the destination display. Summersons took the Hutchinson concern over sometime in 1930 but do not appear to have taken any of their buses on. This vehicle is a Ford Model T and is seen in West Auckland village. *(Summerson Family Collection)*

A group of Eden staff, probably drivers with their conductresses, pose outside one of the company Leyland buses. As mentioned elsewhere, George Summerson was a keen photographer in his spare time and had his own dark room for developing negatives. He would often engage his staff into posing for various photos such as this one. **(Summerson Family Collection)**

approached his father, who duly gave him a £200 loan. George purchased a 14-seat Chevrolet bus, and named it 'The Eden Bus Service' after the Eden House that he lived in. ('Eden' originated from the Eden family, who owned large areas of land, especially around South West Durham). George applied for a licence to run a service from Bishop to West, though the local council insisted he ran to Evenwood so as not to disadvantage the other operators on the route.

A condition of the loan to George was to give his brother William (Bill) a role in the business. Bill at the time was a wagon driver and he would be mainly responsible for the administration of the operation and looking after the cash takings, though other family members, namely brothers Tom, Harry and sister Kate would also gain employment in the operation.

Initially, the base of the operations would be at the family home of Eden House, where the entire family lived together. The scullery was used as an office cum crew rest room, and the buses kept outside when not working.

The Summersons soon became involved in the chaos of the competition of the route and one trick was to turn the bus round at the end of West Auckland if there were no passengers for Evenwood. The crew would watch in the distance for the competition to come into view coming down from Evenwood and then set off, in order to clear up the passengers en route to Bishop Auckland.

The following year, a service was introduced from West Auckland to Spennymoor, in conjunction with another West Auckland bus operator by the name of Hutchinsons. The route took in the railway town of Shildon and several mining communities, but omitting Bishop Auckland town centre itself. Originally planned to extend to Ferryhill, this was one of the rare instances that the local authorities declined a licence due to the intense competition already between Spennymoor and Ferryhill.

It was a clever route; travelling though these densely populated yet isolated communities, the service provided transport for workers to the collieries and the large railway works in Shildon, as well as linking through to Spennymoor which again, like Bishop, was a thriving town with an iron works, and the famous 'Rink', a ballroom where many relationships were formed! The roads used, however, were very poorly maintained, some being little more than mere dirt tracks and the bad condition of the roads played havoc with the rudimentary suspension systems of the buses used. However, the popularity of the service meant that despite this, it was worthwhile to keep the service going, despite the obvious service and repair costs involved.

As the business expanded, the Summersons obtained land just a few hundred yards from the family home and erected a garage, which not only housed the buses but also sold petrol and acted as a motor car servicing and repair business. The Summersons also operated a small number of motor cars, which were used mainly as taxis. Another service provided by the Summersons was the recharging of wireless receiver batteries!

The Government of the time then introduced the 1930 Road Traffic Act, which sought to regulate the provision of bus services across the country. Bishop Auckland was not alone in playing host to the crazy scenes of bus operators competing for business. To summarize, a Traffic Commissioner was established in each area and he or she would issue licences to the bus operators for the services they wished to operate, and to enforce the timetable, so that there would be no more early or late running in order to poach passengers from other operators.

Bus service licences, however, would only be issued usually if there was no other operator on the proposed route and, upon application, there would be a statutory period of time for other operators, including the railway companies, to object to a proposal. Objections would usually be heard at a sitting of the Traffic Commissioner who had the final say as to the issue of the licence, though usually the objectors got their way.

Each licence specified the timetable that the operator had to adhere to, and fares were also set by the commissioner, thus ending the practice of operators under-cutting each other on price. Drivers and conductors also had to apply for licences, and taxes would be payable by the bus operators. This regulation saw off many of the smaller operators.

In the case of the Evenwood-Bishop section, a fifteen minute frequency was imposed, with a turn issued to OK, Anderson of Evenwood (better known as 'Blue Belle', Stephenson of Etherley, and the remaining quarter given between F Lockey & Son and Summersons. It was intended that Lockey would operate the morning portion of this share, and Summerson the afternoon. The arrangement passed to Lockey and Summerson reflected the fact they were the less established operators on the route. This was not an attractive proposition to the Summersons, and they duly sold their share of the route to Lockeys.

The West Auckland to Spennymoor route was uncontested, with Summersons and Hutchinsons becoming joint operators. However, presumably using the money gained from the sale to Lockey of their share in the Bishop-Evenwood service, the Summersons took the Hutchinsons company over, leaving Summerson the sole operator of this route.

Larger and heavier buses, mostly Leylands, were acquired to deal with the increasing passengers and the difficult road conditions.

To demonstrate how important the Spennymoor service was to residents along the route, a section of road from the village of Gurney Valley was in the worst condition; it was unmade, riddled with pot holes and featured a steep climb with a 90 degree bend in between. The residents of the houses up the hill in winter would take their ashes from the coal fires and throw them on the road, to give the buses some extra traction in negotiating the hill.

One of the Eden buses was referred to as the 'Might'etta', reputedly it's hill climbing ability was poor and it was often remarked that on this bus, the passengers might have to (or might'etta!) walk up the bank as the bus could not cope with the load on it! It does seem, however, that most independent bus companies of this time had at least one bus christened 'Might'etta!'

The buses of this time too, were very basic compared to what one might expect nowadays too. Fitted heaters were rare (though the driver was sat next to the engine which provided a

HE 5317 is a Leyland Lion purchased second hand from the Yorkshire Traction company shortly before the outbreak of war. The fearsome starting handle can be seen below the radiator. *(C Mills Collection)*

source of heat, useful in the winter but not so in the summer); power-assisted steering and synchromesh gearboxes were unheard of!

Starting the engine involved turning a large handle at the front by hand, and this was not without its risks, the compression of the engine would often cause the handle to 'kick back' and broken wrists were the usual consequence. One Summersons driver was unfortunately hit full in the face by the handle and knocked his entire row of top teeth out. In the winter, the bus windows would be frozen on the inside as well as out, on those buses that stood outside. However, passengers would board with their old Army issue greatcoats and hob nailed boots and never complain! Winter would also see the engines being started with the aid of a cloth soaked in diesel and placed in a specially made holding device, which was then set alight held over the air inlet. As the engine turned it would draw in the heat and flames to help fire the first compression of the engine.

Drivers were also expected to be conversant in the mechanics of the internal combustion engine, in order to make hasty repairs if needed. The conductor or conductress had a relatively easy task of issuing tickets and taking fares. Tickets were pre-printed, in varying colours to reflect the fare paid. The conductor/ress would take a ticket from the wooden rack, insert it in the punch to mark the point the passenger boarded at, and the operation of the punch rang a small bell to indicate the punch had worked. The small circles were then collected in the punch box and at the end of the shift the colours would be sorted and tallied with the amount of cash taken. These small circles of paper were put to good use as wedding confetti at the wedding of one of the Summerson's staff!

However, the 'duc' as the conductor/ress would be commonly referred to, had to on occasion keep order on the bus, as well as assist in time keeping on the route. This was frequently a problem on the last departure from Spennymoor on a Friday and Saturday night as intoxicated revellers staggered onto the buses and courting couples from the 'Rink' had one last goodnight kiss.....it's unknown how many were left on the kerb and faced a walk home....

Aside from the Spennymoor service, contracts were also obtained from local collieries to transport their staff to and from work. One in particular was the large colliery at Fishburn, who took on a number of redundant miners who had previously worked in pits near to Bishop Auckland. Contracts such as this were highly prized as it provided guaranteed revenue, with payments coming direct from the colliery rather than depending upon passengers catching the bus and paying fares. The garage services were also a good source of revenue as levels of private car ownership saw a modest increase. Within the ten years since inception of the company, George and Bill had slowly built up a healthy business which put them in good stead for the uncertainties of the war years.

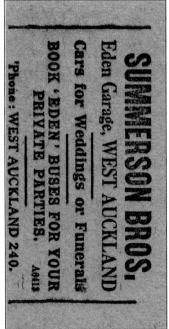

A selection of 'Bell Punch' tickets used by Summerson Brothers. Tickets were stored in a rack and one was taken and placed in a punch which marked the fare stage where the passengers boarded. Operation of the punch sounded a bell, which gave rise to the term 'ringing a ticket out' *(S Gray collection)*

2 – THE 'FORTIES AND 'FIFTIES – WARTIME PROBLEMS AND POST WAR EXPANSION

The onset of war between Britain and Germany presented new challenges to the Summersons. Fuel was rationed, and as a result the West Auckland-Spennymoor service was reduced to cope with this, running approximately every two hours except at peak times for scholars and workers etc. Many operators found their buses requisitioned by the Ministry of Defence and staff were conscripted into the Armed Forces, but it is unknown if the Summersons were affected by this. What is known, is that a 'defence permit' had to be applied for each year to continue running the Spennymoor service.

The Summersons did gain a contract to transport workers to the Royal Ordnance Factory, near Aycliffe. The site, where Aycliffe Business Park is now located, was chosen as it was mainly on marsh land, and often shrouded in fog and mist, thus shielding it from any attacks by the Luftwaffe. The workers were mainly women, and in time became known as the 'Aycliffe Angels'. They made ammunition for the war effort, and work was highly hazardous, as can be expected when handling explosives. The journey to and from work was also not without its risks. Under 'blackout' conditions imposed by the government there were no street lights and vehicles had to have their headlights covered up save for a thin strip, which basically gave no assistance to the driver and only really served as a marker light to warn other vehicles of their presence.

The road towards the factory from Middridge in particular suffered badly with fog and mist and it was not uncommon for the conductor and a few passengers to alight from the bus and walk just in front, to check for obstructions.

Another documented wartime service provided by Summersons was a factory workers service from Ferryhill to the trading estate in St Helen Auckland. There was a large clothing factory here which undertook the manufacture of uniforms for the armed forces. There was also a stage service from Shildon to the village of Middridge some two miles to the east of Shildon.

The Summersons still owned a few cars that were previously used for hire, perhaps similar to a taxi nowadays. The council contracted the Summersons to carry hospital patients, usually those deemed at the time to be 'mentally ill' and also pregnant ladies to maternity hospitals. One can only speculate if any babies made their appearance in the rear of a Summerson's car!

A hearse was also acquired, and drivers were often called upon to help the undertakers with their duties, including putting the deceased bodies in coffins and act as a bearer at the funeral.

The hearse was unusual, in that it had the chassis of a sports car with an ornate, previously horse-drawn hearse body attached to it.

George was appointed Chief Fire Officer for West Auckland during the war, and a fire tender and pump were housed in a garage next to the Old Manor House close to the village centre.

The end of hostilities was to provide new opportunities for the Summerson Brothers. The Royal Ordnance Factory and surrounding areas were converted into factories with new businesses being attracted to the site with readymade buildings and access roads. The area was now known as Aycliffe Trading Estate, named after the village of Aycliffe just to the east.

Aycliffe Village lay on the Great North Road (A1), and was served by United and Northern buses between Newcastle, Durham and Darlington. Summersons were successful in gaining contracts for factory workers to Aycliffe Trading Estate, but applied to operate a stage service between Bishop Auckland and Aycliffe Village, via Shildon and Middridge (replacing the short service introduced earlier) and serving the Trading Estate at shift-change times. This would create a new link for the people of Aycliffe to visit Shildon and Bishop.

It can also be reasonably suspected that Summersons had their eye on the construction of Newton Aycliffe, one of the many new towns envisaged by the Labour government of the time. Newton Aycliffe would lie between Aycliffe Village and Middridge and so be easily served by their buses coming from Aycliffe.

United were also conscious of this new development and indeed, they objected to the Aycliffe service planned by Summersons by saying it would detract their revenue from existing services they operated there, and staked a claim by saying that it was already the established operator in the area. Furthermore, United also operated between Shildon and Bishop Auckland, though one came from the All Saints area of the town and missed out the town centre altogether; the other left Shildon town centre and went on a convoluted route via Eldon.

Not only were objections from United forthcoming, but also from the London North Eastern Railway. There was still a railway station in Aycliffe Village; anyone wanting to travel to Shildon and Bishop Auckland obviously did so by rail, but with a change required in Darlington. Eventually, the three parties, United, the LNER and Summersons, ended up in court, with Summersons being victorious, and a licence for an hourly service was granted.

The Eden route would operate from Shildon town centre, along Main Street and then via Busty Bank, entering Bishop Auckland past Wilson's Forge on South Church Road and terminating at the Grammar School. This made for a very quick journey time into Bishop Auckland as opposed to the United services which operated via Cockton Hill Road. The licence was granted with some conditions, one of which being that Eden had to establish their own stops in Shildon near the King William public house and at the junction of Main Street and Church Street, so as not to 'poach' any intending United passengers.

As Newton Aycliffe was constructed and expanded, the route of the Eden service was altered to take in the new housing areas. United and Northern also developed their services to take in the new town and provide travel opportunities to Durham and Darlington. However, many residents at Newton Aycliffe had moved there from sub-standard housing in Shildon which had been demolished and relied upon The Eden service to enable them to visit family, and continue to shop in the familiar surroundings of Bishop Auckland. A small number of shops had also become established in Newton Aycliffe Town Centre and the Eden service also acted as a local link to connect the housing areas with the shops. As Eden had the monopoly of services from Newton Aycliffe to Shildon and Bishop Auckland, they were also able to set the fares to their liking and the cost was kept quite favourable, in order to retain their passengers and dissuade anyone being lured to Darlington on the United and Northern services.

The Aycliffe service was also timed to connect with the West Auckland-Spennymoor service at Shildon, to provide connections to each end of that route.

Soon after was the introduction of a shopper's service from Shildon to Stockton-on-Tees, in 1950. This ran twice a week on Wednesdays and Saturdays which coincided with the market days in Stockton. Stockton market was renowned at the time for being one of the biggest in the North East and made full use of the long and wide High Street. Regular excursions had been operated by the Summersons previously and the popularity of these trips persuaded them to try a service. Starting at the bottom of Main Street in Shildon (then known as Datton Gates, after the railway crossing there), the bus continued via Middridge, Newton Aycliffe, Aycliffe Village and the villages of Bishopton and Redmarshall. However, the latter two villages were already served by Scurr's Coaches of Stillington and they duly objected to the new Eden service. The only alternative would have been to operate via Sedgefield or the northern area of Darlington and the Traffic Commissioners, sensing objections from operators in those parts, granted the service with a condition that passengers were not permitted to be carried locally between Bishopton and Stockton.

Again, connections were provided at Shildon from the West-Spennymoor service. The Stockton service was an instant success, and duplication was frequently required especially towards Christmas time.

Back at West Auckland, the garage was improved with the construction of a purpose built brick building, retaining the petrol station and motor repair business and offices for the daily administration tasks. Unusually, the main garage was fitted with central heating, with the reasoning being that during cold weather, the bus engines would start easier and with less stress, wear and tear being put upon them. Additionally, it meant that the buses left the garage already warm, and this would be a good selling point to potential early morning customers who may choose an Eden bus over the competition!

Summersons began to acquire and standardise upon a fleet of Leyland and Bedford buses – Leyland buses were noted for being heavy and well built, thus could deal with the arduous conditions of the service work. Bedford buses

THE EDEN BUS SERVICES

BISHOP AUCKLAND – AYCLIFFE VILLAGE

Via. Shildon — Middridge — Newton Aycliffe — Trading Estate

REVISED TIME TABLE

Commencing Sunday, April 1st, 1956

		Monday to Friday				Saturdays			Sundays		
		a.m.		p.m.	p.m.	p.m.	a.m.		p.m.	p.m.		p.m.
BISHOP AUKLAND	Dep.	9.20		8.20	9.20	10.20	9.20		11.20	1.20		10.20
South Church	"	9.23		8.23		10.23	9.23		11.23	1.23		10.23
Shildon (K.Will.)	"	9.30	then	8.30	see	10.30	9.30	then	11.30	1.30	then	10.30
Middridge	"	9.33		8.33		10.33	9.33		11.33	1.33		10.33
Newton Aycliffe	"	9.40	every	8.40		10.40	9.40	every	11.40	1.40	every	10.40
Aycliffe Vill.	"	9.45		8.45	below	–	9.45		–	1.45		10.45
Newton Aycliffe	"	9.51	hour	8.51		10.41	9.51	hour	11.41	1.51	hour	10.51
Middridge	"	9.58		8.58		10.48	9.58		11.48	1.58		10.58
Shildon (K.Will.)	"	10.2	until	9.02		10.52	10.2	until	11.52	2.2	until	11.2
South Church	"	10.9		9.09		–	10.9		–	2.9		11.9
BISHOP AUKLAND	Arr.	10.12		9.12		–	10.12		–	2.12		11.12

The above journeys will operate on a circular route at the Aycliffe End.

The ODD hour from Bishop Aukland via Stephenson Way, St. Cuthbert's Way, N.E. Gate, Aycliffe Village, Police Headquarters, Block & Andersons, St. Cuthbert's Way, Stephenson Way.

The EVEN hour from Bishop Aukland in the opposite direction.

Journeys (Monday to Saturday) in addition to the above which will continue to run via Simpasture Gate and New Lane.

The 8.30 a.m. from Bishop Aukland runs to Police Headquarters.

		a.m.	a.m.	S.O. a.m.	X.S. a.m.	a.m.	X.S. p.m.	SC. p.m.	p.m.	X.S. p.m.
BISHOP AUCKLAND	Dep.	5.20	–	7.20	7.55	8.30	1.20	4.00	–	9.20
South Church	"	5.23	–	7.23	7.58	8.33	1.23	4.3	–	9.23
Shildon (K.Will.)	"	5.33	–	7.30	8.5	8.40	1.33	4.10	5.15	9.33
Middridge	"	5.36	–	7.33	8.8	8.43	1.36	4.13	5.18	9.36
Newton Aycliffe	"	5.43	–	7.40	8.15	8.50	1.43	4.20	5.27	9.43
Trading Estate N.E.G.	"	5.46	–	7.43	8.19	8.55	1.46	–	–	9.46
Kleemans	"	5.50	–	7.47	8.22	–	1.50	–	–	9.50
Aycliffe Village	Arr.	–	–	7.52	8.27	–	1.55	4.25	–	9.55

		X.S.					S.O.			
Aycliffe Village	Dep.	–	–	7.55	8.30	–	2.00	–	–	10.00
Kleemans	"	–	7.25	–	–	–	2.5	2.5	5.30	10.5
Trading Estate N.E.G.	"	–	7.27	8.00	8.35	9.00	2.9	2.9	5.33	10.9
Newton Aycliffe	"	7.00	7.30	8.4	8.39	9.3	2.12	2.12	5.37	10.12
Middridge	"	7.07	7.37	8.11	8.46	9.10	2.19	2.19	5.44	10.19
Shildon (K.Will.)	"	7.11	7.41	8.15	8.50	9.14	2.23	2.23	5.48	10.23
South Church	"	–	7.48	8.22	8.57	9.21	2.30	2.30	–	10.30
BISHOP AUCKLAND	Arr.	–	7.51	8.25	9.00	9.24	2.33	2.33	–	10.33

S.O. – Saturdays Only: X.S. Except Saturdays: Sc. – School days Only.

This service operates into Bishop Aukland Market Place until 9.0. a.m., after this time Belvedere is the terminus.

A duplicate bus on the 8.30 a.m. from Aycliffe to Shildon will run through Shildon via the Timothy Hackworth School on School days for the purpose of dropping children at this point.

Aycliffe Timetable – The timetable for the Bishop Auckland-Newton Aycliffe service effective from April 1956. The revisions were probably made to serve a recently constructed part of Newton Aycliffe. In time, the Aycliffe service was enhanced to a thirty minute frequency through the day, Monday to Saturday. George Summerson had his own printing press with which he used to print company timetables.

HUP 314, another Leyland Tiger with Duple bodywork, is seen at Spennymoor having travelled here from West Auckland. The crew have their backs to the photographer and appear to be taking a short break from their duties. *(Unknown copyright)*

GTC 975, a Leyland Tiger with Roe bodywork enters Stockton High Street on the market day service from Shildon. A Bee-Line Roadways coach follows close behind as Stockton Corporation vehicles pass in the opposite direction. *(Unknown copyright)*

KUP 747 is a Leyland Tiger PS2 with Gurney Nutting coachwork, purchased new by the Summersons in 1949. The actual date of the photo is unknown but presumably the coach has been used to transport supporters of Bishop Auckland F.C. to see them compete in one of their famous FA Amateur Cup victories in 1955, 1956 or 1957. *(Unknown copyright)*

George Lowes (left) and Tom Summerson (right) complete paperwork in the office at West Auckland. *(Summerson Family Collection)*

HVO 126, a Leyland Tiger PS2 with Duple bodywork is seen outside the lower garage at West Auckland. This was a secondhand acquisition from an operator in Hull. The rugged heavyweight Leyland chassis was ideal for the service bus operations and the coach seats would have been appreciated by the loyal Eden passengers, but also meant that the bus could be used on private hire and excursion work if needed. *(Gordon Wigham Collection)*

were cheap to buy and run, and were used mainly on contract work. The livery used at this time was a smart deep red, almost crimson with a maroon relief on the skirts of the buses.

Buses were usually still of a traditional 'half cab' design, where the driver sat next to the engine at the front. A Leyland 'Royal Tiger' was purchased new in 1951, full fronted with a centre doorway and underfloor-engine. Despite its modern looks, it was unpopular with drivers and returned poor fuel consumption, and it was swiftly sold on.

Interest from United

In November 1954, United management had heard a rumour that the Summersons were considering disposing of their business. George was invited to the United head office in Darlington and he confirmed that he and his brother felt that the business had "reached a turning point", and it was obvious that to continue to develop the bus side of the operation was going to require a large amount of capital in the form of larger vehicles.

Therefore, if they were to be offered a price for the business which they considered satisfactory, then they would indeed sell.

A United memorandum states that at the time, the Summersons owned fifteen vehicles, and George valued them at £20,000. United at this time operated a highly standardised fleet of Bristol buses, and it is remarked that the buses "would be unlikely to be of much use to us".

George supplied United with a week's receipts from the stage carriage services, which showed the business turning a moderate profit. The author of the memo does make specific mention of the Aycliffe service and how if United were to extend it to Darlington it would complement their existing service 1. Further mention is made of a service operating between Darlington and Heighington via Newton Aycliffe provided by Scott's Greys coaches and that if the Summersons were to sell to Scotts Greys this would be a disadvantage to United. Therefore, it would be in the interests of United to purchase the Summersons business.

Negotiations appear to have become protracted and a letter sent by George to the United secretary,

An aerial view of the Eden garage and premises taken in the late 1950s. The large building was the garage used to house and maintain the buses. *(Summerson Family Collection)*

A view of the newly constructed office block and the petrol pumps which dispensed fuel for sale to the public. *(Summerson Family Collection)*

Mr Pratt, mentions that the Summerson's staff were becoming suspicious of United taking over and Bill was concerned about the staff becoming upset. This letter also shows that Bill spent more time with the driving staff, as he was responsible for allocating their duties.

The next record in these discussions is dated 2nd July 1955, which are minutes from a meeting held again at United Head Office, between Mr Pratt, Mr Deacon (United's general manager) and George. George had said that he and Bill would want £60,000 for the business, comprising £20,000 for the vehicles and £40,000 goodwill. Mr Pratt said that United were thinking somewhere in the region of £25,000 goodwill and £12,000 for the vehicles, of which United would not operate anyway.

George said that he thought this would be the position that United would find themselves in and asked them to realise that the business was profitable and showing improvement year on year. With this in mind, he could not be expected to part

with the business for anything other than a very good price.

At this point, negotiations were terminated, though Mr Deacon asked that should the Summersons at any later date think about selling up again, then United should get first refusal to which George agreed, though if someone came along with the £60,000 he thought the company was worth, then it would be sold to that person!

The Petrol Station

Whilst the bus and coach operations were proving to be very profitable, the motor garage business was still an important source of revenue to the Summersons. As private ownership of the motor car increased, so did the sale of petrol and the garage lay on the main road to Barnard Castle and onward to the Pennines.

Durham County Council proposed in the 1950s to build a by-pass road, taking the traffic away from West Auckland. However, the plan

HD 7846, a Leyland Tiger PS1 with Brush bodywork was one of a pair acquired in the late 1950s, second hand from a Yorkshire operator. This was amongst the last of the traditional front engine, half cab buses Summersons operated. *(Gordon Wigham Collection)*

of the new road would have taken traffic away from the garage by little more than 100 yards. This concerned the Summersons, as passing trade would now be lost.

These concerns were further compounded when a Mr Peddlety applied for planning permission to erect and establish a fuel filling station up the road from the Summersons garage, which crucially would have taken the passing trade. Incensed by this application, the Summersons appealed to the Council and applied to move their filling station opposite the site proposed by Peddlety! In a letter to the surveyors of the Barnard Castle Rural District Council (who were responsible for building matters), George Summerson cited that the business had been selling fuel at that location for almost thirty years. The Summersons application and subsequent appeals were all declined, and Peddlety was allowed to establish his business – as it transpired, however, the building of the by-pass would not happen for almost another fifty years.

3 – INTO THE 'SWINGING SIXTIES'

The Summersons business continued to flourish into the 1960s. The Aycliffe service was doubled in frequency to run every thirty minutes during the day from Monday to Saturday. However, this was not without continued opposition from United as now The Eden were also running every half hour between Shildon and Bishop Auckland. The Summersons were able to demonstrate that a half hourly service was necessary to cope with demand and the Commissioners accepted the extension.

Two new factory services were also licenced by the Commissioners, operating again from Aycliffe Trading Estate to Shildon, with one continuing to Leeholme and the other to West Auckland. This perhaps indicates the closure of factories and collieries, and new jobs being created at the rapidly expanding Aycliffe Trading Estate. These 'factory' services also served the huge railway workshops at Shildon.

There was a peculiar and unofficial seating arrangement on the 'factory' services. The regular passengers had what they deemed to be their own seats, and unsuspecting passengers on their way to their first day at work would be told in no uncertain terms that they were occupying someone else's seat! The conductress would usually turn a blind eye to these proceedings.....

The early 1960s saw a small change to the West Auckland-Spennymoor service. Spennymoor itself was burdened with a large amount of sub standard housing in the town and the area known as Low Spennymoor was earmarked for industrial redevelopment. To alleviate this, the local council of the time embarked upon the construction of a large housing estate in the area known as Middlestone Moor, roughly one mile to the south of Spennymoor. The Summersons were able to divert the Spennymoor service to take in the estate and bring in some extra revenue for the service, which was suffering from a decline due to the reducing amount of industry along the route.

The design of buses and coaches was evolving as well. The fashion of the time was to put the engine and gearbox underneath the bus, usually half way along the chassis. The bodybuilders responded to this with modern designs and almost universally placed the doors alongside the driver.

This meant that the conductor or conductress could now concentrate exclusively on collecting fares and the driver could supervise boarding and alighting.

Leyland and Bedford were still the preferred choice of the Summersons and after the experience of the Royal Tiger, Leyland introduced the 'Tiger Cub' which had a lighter chassis construction method as opposed to the Royal Tiger and used a smaller engine, which was more fuel efficient. The first Tiger Cubs were actually acquired in the late 1950s and Summersons gave their Cubs a fleet number as an easy way of identification – for example the first, TUP 778 was numbered 'C1' or 'Cub 1'.

Bedford buses and coaches were usually bought new, ran for a few years and then sold on. Bedford chassis had the engine at the front, but the coachbuilders were still able to make a modern full front design with the door just slightly behind the cab area, but still able to be operated and supervised by the driver. Petrol engines were specified for the Bedford coaches. However, the fuel consumption of these would have been inferior compared to the diesel engine vehicles and this no doubt condemned them to a short working life with the Summersons.

In 1965, George's son David joined the business, after serving a five year apprenticeship with United at their Central Works in Darlington. Like his father, David obtained membership of the Institute of the Motor Industry and of the Institute of Road Transport Engineers through further study at Gateshead Motor Vehicle College. In the first week of David's 21st birthday, he also successfully obtained his Public Service Vehicle (PSV) driving licence. David eventually became the Workshop Manager with the company and eventually a Company Director.

Leyland had also introduced their new bus chassis to replace the Royal Tiger, named the Leopard. The law had been changed to permit longer lengths of buses and coaches and the Leopard was initially available as a 30ft vehicle to seat an average of 45. The first Leopards came to the company as a result of a travelling salesman who was trying to offload two Leopards ordered by a Scottish company but cancelled after build. An Eden employee jumped in the cab to take the demonstration vehicle on a test drive. As he released the clutch, the 'bite' took him by surprise

Tom Summerson poses with newly purchased Bedford SB/Duple Midland XUP 629. Though the engine is still situated in the front of the vehicle, coachbuilders of the time were able to design a modern looking bus which complemented other designs where the engine was mounted underfloor, and mid-way along the chassis which were gaining popularity at the time. *(Summerson Family Collection)*

George Summerson standing proudly with TUP 778, the first Leyland Tiger Cub purchased new with Burlingham bodywork. This would gain the fleet number C1 or 'Cub 1'. *(Summerson Family Collection)*

XHN 48 was a Bedford SB with Duple coachwork. Bedfords were lighter in construction than Leylands and most were fitted with a petrol engine. They rarely saw use on normal service work and were usually sold on after a couple of years' service. *(Gordon Wigham Collection)*

LNY 363 was one of a pair of Leyland Royal Tigers with Weymann bodywork acquired in 1963 from an operator in South Wales. They turned out to be a bit of a dud purchase, the Royal Tigers were unpopular with the drivers as they were extremely heavy, and with the weight came poor fuel consumption. They were swiftly withdrawn! *(Gordon Wigham Collection)*

36 CPT, a Bedford SB with Yeates of Loughborough coachwork. In what looks to be a busy summer afternoon in Scarborough working either an excursion or private hire. *(Gordon Wigham Collection)*

1825 PT, a Bedford SB1 with Duple Midland bodywork. Summersons took delivery of this in 1961 but the bus was previously exhibited at the 1960 Commercial Motor Show. Several of these Bedfords were bought new and put to use on the West Auckland-Spennymoor service, though as with most Bedfords they were not retained long. *(Gordon Wigham Collection)*

XHN 48, a Bedford SB/Duple, with the future company directors posing! Barry, son of Bill, is the smart young man outside and David, son of George is the boy standing in the doors of the coach. **(Summerson Family Collection)**

and the bus lurched forward, almost crashing into the garage wall! The decision, however, was taken there and then to acquire these two buses, which were offered at an attractive price and they gained the fleet numbers L1 and L2. Although the Leopard had a larger engine than the Tiger Cubs, they were remarkably economical and extremely reliable and L1/2 were usually found hard at work on the Bishop-Aycliffe service.

The mid 1960s saw a change to the fleet livery used for the buses. The traditional red and maroon gave way to a brighter red and ivory scheme which gave a fresher and more modern look to the vehicles.

Further investment to the service bus fleet came towards the end of the decade. The coachbuilders Plaxton of Scarborough were particularly popular with the independent bus and coach operators of the North East of England, and their 'Highway' design was a common sight – Summersons had already purchased a sole example of a Highway on a Tiger Cub chassis.

Plaxton replaced the Highway design with a new 'Derwent' body. George was invited to the Plaxton factory in Scarborough to give his views

and input to the design of the Derwent. Indeed, the Summersons ordered two on Bedford VAM chassis. The VAM was the best of both worlds for the Summersons as it combined familiar Bedford engineering with a Leyland diesel engine. One of the buses was used extensively in Plaxton publicity before use by the Summersons.

A pair of relatively youthful Leyland Leopards were also acquired from Weardale Motor Services. The Summersons had forged a close working relationship with the Gibson family who operated the Weardale company and the two companies often loaned each other buses and coaches. The influx of these heavier Leyland vehicles began to see off the older Bedford buses and further modernise the fleet.

Providing additional capacity on the Bishop-Aycliffe service was becoming a problem; duplicate buses were frequently needed and this needed extra crews to operate them. The late 1960s were a particularly difficult time for bus operators who were faced with chronic staff shortages and the extra crews required was a burden. Double-deckers could not be operated, due to the layout of the garage (it wasn't high enough!) and a few low

LPT 337C is a Leyland Leopard with Willowbrook bodywork, one of a pair purchased as a result of a cancelled order from an operator in Scotland. Initially operated in the livery they were purchased in they were soon repainted into the new Eden livery style. *(Unknown copyright)*

L8 (RUP 6D) was a Leyland Leopard with Plaxton Highway bodywork, acquired from nearby Weardale Motor Services. This was another 55-seater and was usually driven by Alan Murgatroyd who treated the vehicle as if it was his own. *(Unknown copyright)*

railway bridges in areas served excluded their use anyway. However, the law was changed further to permit buses and coaches being built to a length of 36ft, and the first bus purchased by The Eden to this specification was another Leyland Leopard, with Plaxton Derwent bodywork, which seated 55 people.

Most of the Eden drivers had never handled something of such length, and initially it was an unpopular machine. Although bus design had come a long way since 1927, this and the other Leopards had no power steering and a constant mesh or 'crash' gearbox which could be difficult to master, though from an engineer's view it was simpler to maintain.

The end of the 1960s saw Bill's son Barry join the family business. Barry had trained as an accountant and had been employed latterly by Smart & Browns, who had established a large factory in Spennymoor and produced home electrical goods such as cookers and refrigerators. Barry became office and transport manager, before also becoming a company director with his cousin David.

The first bus purchased new by the Summersons to the maximum permitted length of 36 feet was L5 (EPT 615G). Normally allocated to the Bishop Auckland-Aycliffe service it is seen here at the garage. *(Unknown copyright)*

4 – THE 1970S – BUILDING A MODERN FLEET

As the Summersons business entered the 1970s, they were struggling against the availability of staff and the rising levels of car ownership. Although the practise of 'one man operation' was coming into vogue, the Summersons preferred to keep with the tradition of employing conductors or conductresses to collect the fares on the bus.

The government in the late 1960s had introduced the New Bus Grant scheme, which providing the bus was built to a specific design qualified for a discount on purchase, the shortfall coming from the tax-payer. It was also possible to get coaches on this scheme, though each vehicle had to spend a certain amount of time on stage carriage service, and they were designed accordingly. Commonly known as 'dual purpose' vehicles, they looked to all intents and purposes as a coach but featured destination displays and a particular type of entrance/exit door. Service buses also qualified for the grant, initially set at 25% of the purchase price, to help operators modernise their fleet.

Capacity was still a problem on the Bishop-Aycliffe service, and three further Leyland Leopards were taken into the fleet. Two came second hand, once again from Weardale Motor Services, with Plaxton Highway bodies, with a seating capacity of 55. The other was brand new to the Summersons and came in the form of L7 (LPT 665J), which was similar to L5 but featured some new technology to the Eden drivers in the form of a semi-automatic gearbox.

A semi-automatic gearbox dispensed with the use of a clutch, and meant that the difficult skill of mastering double de-clutch gearchanges was not needed. The Eden drivers were not keen on it, however, and felt it took something out of the job. Nevertheless, the four 55-seaters were now a common feature on the Aycliffe service, and as duplication was not often required, it saved additional costs with fuel and staffing.

It was also around this time that Aycliffe Village was no longer served, save for some journeys in the morning and evening to cater for commuters. Buses instead operated a circular route in Newton Aycliffe and extra services ran on a Thursday, Friday and Saturday to deal with shoppers – Thursday and Saturday were Market days in Bishop.

More Plaxton Derwent buses were bought, but on Bedford chassis, mainly for the Spennymoor service. This influx of new service buses modernised the Eden fleet at a stroke, and using the Derwent body provided a uniform image to the travelling public. Though route numbers were not in use, an illuminated 'EDEN' sign was placed where a route number would usually be found, and placed kerb side for easy identification. The coaches were used on the Aycliffe Trading Estate services, and additionally on private hires and excursions to satisfy the terms of the bus grant.

Sadly in 1976, Bill Summerson died, and the decision was made then to create a new limited company, Eden Bus Services Ltd, still trading as The Eden, with David, Barry and George listed as directors.

Durham County Council at this time also started to take a pro-active interest in the local bus operations in the county. One of the innovations was to introduce a route numbering scheme. Many independent bus operators did not have a route number for their services, and The Eden was no exception, merely showing a destination with little or no detail to the route taken. Durham County Council assigned the following numbers to the following Eden routes.

Bishop Auckland-Newton Aycliffe *became 91 and 92, the differing numbers to distinguish which direction each route took around Newton Aycliffe.*

Bishop Auckland-Aycliffe Village *became 93- this was the morning/afternoon service that also served the Trading Estate.*

West Auckland to Spennymoor *became 99*

Shildon to Stockton *became 165*

West Auckland to Aycliffe Trading Estate *became 961*

Leeholme to Aycliffe Trading Estate *became 962.*

Despite service numbers being allocated, the public rarely referred to them as they would with say United. It was common for people to speak of a certain United service by referring to the service number, but with an Eden service virtually everybody would say "we'll get The Eden!"

A further batch of four Leyland Leopards with Plaxton Derwent bodies were in build, to

Q3 (VUP 637L), a Bedford YRQ with Plaxton Elite coachwork, was purchased under the terms of the New Bus Grant. When not used on contracts and private hires it could usually be found on the Aycliffe Industrial Estate and the Stockton market day services, Q3 featured a device which closed the doors when the clutch was depressed, a feature that caused several near misses with alighting passengers if the driver was keen to get away!
(S Gray collection)

become L10,11,12 and 14 – 13 was not used for superstitious reasons! L12 and L14 were specified to be fitted with a service number indicator on the destination display, but rather than use the glass that proudly showed the Eden logo, a thin strip was placed to the left of the destination display. An Eden driver, who went down to Plaxton at Scarborough to collect L12 noticed this feature and informed the Plaxton man that it must be a mistake, as The Eden didn't use service numbers – it was removed without checking and duly driven back to West Auckland, only for David Summerson to remark that they had omitted fitting the service number display, and off it went back to Scarborough! L12 and L14 were also the first Leopards to be provided with power steering, and the semi-automatic gearbox was by now standard on all Leyland Leopards.

1977 saw the company mark their 50th anniversary with a full page advert in the Northern Echo. A development with the Bishop services came in 1978. Bishop had a number of terminuses in the town used by different operators and routes, and all of the companies pressed Durham County Council to allow all the services to use the Market Place as the terminus. As the council were trying to promote co-ordinated bus travel, this seemed a logical thing to do. For example, someone travelling from Newton Aycliffe on the Eden service would be deposited outside the Grammar School, and if they wanted to go to Crook then they would have to walk the fair distance to Bondgate, just up from the OK depot.

However, the council declined this request, saying it would cause too much congestion in the Market Place, which was also the main road

B3 (SFJ 123R) was one of a pair of Bristol LHs with Plaxton Supreme bodywork, acquired in 1986 to help bolster the fleet with the successful bids for local bus services operated on tender to Durham County Council. They were short lived in The Eden fleet and replaced with brand new MCW Metrorider mini coaches. B3 is seen here leaving Bishop Auckland en route to Ferryhill on service 3C. *(C Strong Collection)*

A line up of Plaxton Derwent-bodied Leyland Leopards in the yard at West Auckland. The additional blind for displaying the service number can be seen on three of the vehicles. Other buses without that feature would have blinds made by United at their Central Works which incorporated the route number. *(S Gray collection)*

through the town for all traffic. The combined operators appealed to the Traffic Commissioner who saw that it was indeed a good idea and used their power to overturn the decision of the Council.

At the same time, Eden applied to vary the route of service 92 and it began to operate along Cockton Hill Road and St Andrews Road in Bishop Auckland, in order to serve the hospital. The Commissioner agreed, despite the inevitable protest from United. The routes were also amended in Newton Aycliffe to take in the new Burnhill Way development.

The next purchases by The Eden were a number of Leyland Leopards with coach bodies by Duple. Built in Duple's Blackpool factory, the driver assigned to collect them would be sent down on the passing Primrose service. (Incidentally, collections from Plaxton at Scarborough were usually timed to correspond with a day trip being operated by OK; The Eden were agents for both OK and Primrose and sold their tickets from the office at West Auckland).

Again, they were built to satisfy the requirements of the New Bus Grant and they became stalwarts of The Eden fleet. Unusually though, there was no provision to display a service number. The odd one out was L18 which came with a Plaxton body, though it caught fire one night at Kirk Merrington on the Spennymoor service when still fairly new and it was rebodied by Plaxton with the updated style of 'Supreme' bodywork. Part of the order for Leyland Leopards included another Plaxton Derwent service bus, L15 (ABR 778S), which became the last of that design of Derwent to be built.

It was also customary to 'run in' new buses and coaches on the Spennymoor service, as the timings were fairly slack, one driver in particular noted for having a very light right foot! If there were any problems, then the bus could easily be replaced at the garage in West Auckland.

The influx of Leopard coaches saw off the majority of the Bedford buses. The Eden found the Leopard to be a reliable, economical vehicle suitable for all of their work, be it service, contract or excursion. With a modern fleet of vehicles, the company was well prepared for the challenges the 1980s would bring.

L20 (OGR 893T) is a Leyland Leopard with Duple Dominant 2 coach body, seen in Newton Aycliffe on service 93. The handsome lines of the Duple Dominant were enhanced with the liberal application of chrome trim, though in later years the chrome would be removed as it was found to trap moisture and encourage corrosion of the body frames. *(S Gray Collection)*

5 – 1980-1985 – EXPANSION IN COACHING

The Eden had decided to try and expand in the coaching market, of which many regulations were lifted as a result of the 1980 Transport Act. For the first time, a manager was recruited from outside the Summerson family and he tried several exercises to build the private hire side of the operation.

The Eden lacked anything to suit smaller parties and a Bristol LHS coach was purchased, the first Bristol bus in the fleet. It seated 28, and was fitted inside with tables and lamps! It also wore a variation to the red and ivory livery and was branded as the 'Mini-Exec'.

Leopard coach L22 was branded as a 'Maxi-Exec', again with tables fitted and other touches intended to create an air of luxury. However, to satisfy the terms of the bus grant it still had to work on normal service and so passengers would occasionally be treated to something quite plush for their usual journey!

Another first for The Eden, was the purchase of a striking Volvo B58 coach. Eden had previously used a similar vehicle on demonstration, though with Belgian made Van Hool coachwork. The coach they purchased, however, became V1 (LTN 753X) and had coachwork by Duple to their 'Dominant 3' design. It had trapezoid windows and literally turned heads with its American inspired design. As it was again purchased under the terms of the bus grant, it was designed to be used also on local service work and certainly caused a stir when it was.

V1 was branded as the 'Video Executive', and was fitted with a television and video cassette player; sadly these features were not used when on service work!

Although L22 and V1 had to spend spells operating on the stage carriage work, this was not seen as a bad thing as passengers could appreciate the luxury touches to these coaches first hand, and then if they needed to hire a coach could ask for it by name when applying.

The private hire business did quite well as a result, but not without incident. One evening, a coach was booked to pick up revellers from the

A new manager sought to build the private hire aspect of the business and this Bristol LHS mini coach was purchased. B1 (XFP 489S) was branded as the 'Mini-Exec' and featured tables with lamps. B1 gained the nickname of 'Puddle Jumper' as a reference to the ride characteristics of the basic leaf sprung chassis *(S Gray collection)*

To compliment the 'Mini-Exec', there was also a 'Maxi-Exec', a job given to L22 (TUP 921V), a Leyland Leopard with Duple Dominant 2 coachwork. Again fitted with tables, curtains and other luxurious touches it is seen in Newton Aycliffe giving a touch of class to recently introduced service 93 from West Auckland to Newton Aycliffe. (*S Gray collection*)

LT1 (TTY 841Y) was the last Leyland to be purchased new by The Eden. It is a Leyland Tiger with a Plaxton Paramount 3200 body and was fitted with a toilet and television with a video player. LT1 spent a lot of time operating tours in Continental Europe when new. *(S Gray collection)*

.Top Hat nightclub in Spennymoor. The driver was impatient to leave and was continually prevented by some vociferous members of those already on board as some of the party were still in the Top Hat. The driver then went inside the club to chase the tardy members of the party onto the coach, but when he went back outside, the coach had gone! It was found a few days later, and it transpired that one of the passengers on the coach was also becoming impatient, and decided to drive it home himself.

Changes to the Local Services

The early 1980s saw the first major change to the long established 99 service, from West Auckland to Spennymoor. The service was split at Shildon, to operate between Shildon and Spennymoor only. This presented a problem as there was nowhere suitable to turn the bus around in Shildon at the time. An application to operate a loop around Central Parade and Byerley Road was declined and thus the bus used a side street just off Main Street.

Eden were also looking at Woodhouse Close Estate, just off Tindale Crescent on the 99 route. A new service from Woodhouse to Newton Aycliffe was experimented which took up the 93 route number. This was extended to West Auckland to replace the Shildon-West Auckland section of the 99. Eden now had three buses an hour between Shildon and Newton Aycliffe, though the 93 was not particularly efficient in terms of operation. It used two buses and had a lengthy layover in Newton Aycliffe whereby the bus was not in service but the staff still had to be paid. The 93 was subsequently dropped as a result and the 99 returned to its original route, though every other hour served Woodhouse Close as passenger numbers and demand for travel to Shildon from there was encouraging.

It was also at this time that The Eden converted to full 'one person operation', and the conductresses were either made redundant or offered other jobs within the company. Some of the Eden 'ducs' at this time had a formidable reputation; one would berate the driver in front of

M1 (369 EBC) was an impressive Mercedes-Benz O.303 coach which was initially used as a demonstrator. It took over much of the Continental tour work that The Eden operated at the time. The driver is Chris Johnson, who was another long standing Eden employee and began work there at leaving school. *(A Jarosz)*

his passengers if his driving skills left something to be desired. Another would bring a feast of homemade pies and pastries for her driver. The 'ducs' would also be on first name terms with many of the passengers. There was an outcry when the 'ducs' were removed from service, but from a business point of view it improved the profits of the service work by removing a wage from the running costs.

1983 saw the purchase of the last brand new Leyland by The Eden. This was a Leyland Tiger, the Tiger being the replacement for the venerable Leopard design. It was branded as the 'Video Eurocruiser', and with it came package trips to Europe. Again, a television and video cassette player were fitted, though in time a toilet was also installed. The Tiger (numbered LT1) also found itself on normal service work, though the toilet was locked out of use!

1984 saw two further Leyland Leopards enter the fleet, one from Trimdon Motor Services which had coach seats but were replaced with bus style seating by The Eden, and another with Alexander bodywork from the Tyne and Wear PTE. This was an unusual 62-seater, with three plus two seating, and was acquired to operate a contract tendered by Barnard Castle School for a daily scholars service from Darlington.

The Tiger was complemented on the European work by a magnificent Mercedes-Benz coach. It was used as a demonstrator and came fully loaded with a television, toilet and hot drink making facilities. An 'Eden Holidays' unit was set up, with a dedicated office and staff, and they were marketed in the local press. The Mercedes was purchased at a keen price and offered some competition to neighbouring OK Motor Services, who also offered a package coach tour programme but didn't have anything like the 'Merc' amongst their coaches.

1985 saw the introduction of a staff uniform, a smart maroon blazer with cream shirt, maroon tie and epaulettes. A driver was also promoted to the task of being an inspector, and travelled around the Eden network checking tickets, punctuality and dealing with any problems that may occur on the service routes.

6 – COMPETITION AND CO-OPERATION

The 1985 Transport Act called for the de-regulation of the bus industry, ending the strict regulation of bus services and making an almost free market for bus operators. Bus companies could operate on whichever route they chose regardless of any existing operator on that route. County councils were also required to subsidise routes that would not make a profit were it to be run 'commercially', ie operated at the financial risk of an operator, and put out to competitive tender by the council.

The Act also called for the privatisation of the National Bus Company, of which United was a part. The individual companies were to be sold off to the private sector; United was one of a few deemed to be too large to sell off as it stood and it was broken up prior to sale, the operations in Tyneside and Northumberland formed the new Northumbria Motor Services company, and the operations in Scarborough passed to East Yorkshire Motor Services to become Scarborough and District.

United was, therefore, left with the County Durham, Cleveland and North Yorkshire parts of its operation. The Eden teamed up with a local estate agent, Trevor Southern, and made a bid for the United company – however, they were unsuccessful and United was acquired by Caldaire Holdings who had also purchased another former National Bus Company subsidiary in Yorkshire.

The Eden had to look at their current operations and decide which they could afford to run at a commercial risk, with the deadline for the new services to start on the 26th October 1986. Meanwhile, United had amassed a large fleet of minibuses and some of these were to be put into use in Darlington, to compete against Darlington Transport (DTC), the council owned company who provided all the town services in Darlington.

The Eden were then also informed by United that they intended to register a service 14, running from Bishop Auckland to Darlington via Shildon and Newton Aycliffe. United were finally able to retaliate against the Bishop-Aycliffe service that the Summersons had introduced over thirty years previously.

The net result of this was a collaboration between The Eden and Darlington Transport. DTC wished to compete with the out of town services provided by United from Darlington, and The Eden wished to protect its revenue on their lucrative 91/92 services. A network of jointly operated services was established, under the 'Dart' brand. The Eden would provide a matching frequency between Bishop Auckland and Darlington via Shildon and Newton Aycliffe, whereas DTC would operate a 20 minute frequency between Newton Aycliffe and Darlington, combining to provide a ten minute frequency between Newton Aycliffe and Darlington. Fares were agreed upon and return tickets issued by The Eden were available for travel back on a DTC bus, and vice-versa.

The three Eden services, 91, 92 and 93, provided a bus for the first time from Shildon town centre and Jubilee Estate to Darlington. Previous to this, the only way to Darlington by bus was to go to either the Byerley Road or New Shildon areas of town.

There was extensive local media advertising for the routes. Eden preferred to use their fleet of Duple Dominant-bodied Leyland Leopards on the new services as the coach seats provided a touch of comfort for the passengers. DTC acquired similar buses second hand to compliment The Eden's!

L21 (RGR 756V) is seen in Bishop Auckland bus station loading passengers before setting off for Newton Aycliffe. This, and another of the Duple Dominant-bodied Leyland Leopards, carried an experimental livery style that was swiftly discontinued. *(S Gray collection)*

The Dart services were permitted to start just ahead of de-regulation day. Initially, the service was quiet between Newton Aycliffe and Darlington, but the timetable was left untouched in order to help passengers become familiar with it, and by Christmas 1986 the Dart network was proving to be very popular indeed. United kept changing their timetables at short notice, as the Act permitted any operator to do so if they wished, but the travelling public appreciated the stability of the Dart services and thus built up a loyal customer base.

Service 99 was left virtually unaltered and suffered little competition, save for Middlestone Moor, when United altered the route of its service 2 to serve the estate. Service 165 on a Wednesday was again unaltered, but the restriction of picking up passengers in Bishopton and Redmarshall was lifted under the terms of the new Transport Act. The Saturday 165 service was replaced by a new X65, operating from West Auckland to

Shildon, then Newton Aycliffe and then using the A66 to reach Stockton and terminating in Middlesbrough. This was an immediate success and complemented one of the DTC routes from Aycliffe which carried onto Middlesbrough from Darlington.

The United service 14 was short lived, and replaced in time with the X14, an hourly service from Bishop Auckland to Middlesbrough via Shildon and Darlington. It used dedicated drivers and coaches and did take some of the Eden's custom from Shildon and Jubilee Estate, attracted no doubt by the very quick travel times to Darlington. The United service 4 was left to compete against The Eden between Bishop Auckland and Newton Aycliffe. This led Durham County Council to advise in their timetables booklets to contact the respective operator before you travelled to check the current schedule, owing to the intense competition between the two operators.

The Eden successfully tendered for a town service route in Birtley from the Tyne and Wear Passenger Transport Executive. The route involved some narrow housing estate roads and thus two Freight Rover Sherpa minibuses with Dormobile bodywork were acquired from Midland Red West. S2 (D70 YRF) is seen here on service 23. *(G Stainthorpe)*

The last buses purchased new by The Eden were a trio of MCW Metrorider minibuses. They seated 33 and featured coach seating. MR1 (F201 RVN) is seen in Middlesbrough when still new about to return to West Auckland (not Bishop, as the destination blind says!) on service X65. *(Ian Wilson)*

The Eden were successful in gaining some tendered work from Durham County Council. One contract was to provide a bus service to the village of Leasingthorne, between Coundon and Kirk Merrington. This became service 3C, and ran from Bishop Auckland to Ferryhill. The 3C became a popular service and was eventually operated without subsidy. It took passengers from the competing United service between Bishop and Ferryhill, and some minor alterations were made to the route to take in Leeholme and continue to Wood Lane Estate in Ferryhill.

Another tender gain took The Eden well away from their established operating area. The contract was won to operate service 7 on a Sunday, between Bishop and Wheatley Hill, a former mining community near Peterlee. The route had its origins in the Gillet Brothers service from Hartlepool to Bishop Auckland that United acquired when it bought the Gillet business out in 1974. (United operated the weekday service commercially).

1988 saw what would be the last new vehicle purchase made by the Summerson family. A trio of MCW 'Metrorider' minibuses were purchased. They were a purpose built small bus, with 33 coach seats and the novelty for an Eden driver of an automatic gearbox!

Yet another departure away from the traditional operating area was the successful tender for a town service in Birtley, near Gateshead. This tender came from the Tyne and Wear Passenger Transport Executive and required a small minibus in order to negotiate certain parts of the route. Two Freight Rover Sherpas were purchased and kept at the English Mustard factory in Birtley. The Sherpa minibuses were small 16-seat van conversions and were not particularly popular with the driving staff when they occasionally ventured out into service from West Auckland. The author recalls their use on service 99 on a Wednesday afternoon when it was half day closing in Spennymoor, and passenger numbers were low. The Birtley contract was short lived and the Sherpas found their way onto another tender gain, this time in Darlington on a town service.

In order to modernise the fleet, five second hand Leyland National buses were acquired, fitted with Volvo engines in place of the original Leyland 510 unit and had their ages disguised with Northern Ireland registration plates. The quintet are seen here posed in front of the Eden garage. *(Steve Foster)*

7 – MORE COMPETITION AND THE END?

The Eden entered the 1990s in a reasonably fit state, the service network was performing well, and in the face of continued competition from United, Eden enjoyed a large and loyal customer base.

Eden continued to pick up tendered work from Durham County Council that was well outside the traditional operating area. The tender for the town service in Birtley was lost but work for the Sherpa minibuses was found in the form of two rural services from Durham City, one to Burnhope and another to East Hedleyhope. Other work came in the form of a temporary service from Durham to Sunderland, which was operated in conjunction with Scarlet Band and Bell Brothers of Spennymoor, which was hastily put into place when the incumbent operator, Go-Ahead Northern suffered industrial action from its drivers.

United's parent company Caldaire had acquired Trimdon Motor Services in 1990, and then also approached The Eden with a view to a possible takeover. United's services were suffering with the competition provided by the Dart services and were they to take Eden over, then Darlington Transport would have probably pulled out of their competing Darlington-Newton Aycliffe route. However, the Monopolies and Mergers Commission blocked the sale, citing it would remove competition in the market in these areas.

General hostilities between Eden and United seemed to subside slightly until September 1992, when The Eden announced the introduction of new services 1C and 4C. Directly in competition with United, service 1C ran from Crook to Shildon via Bishop Auckland, returning to Bishop as a 4C in a through loop. Service 3C was enhanced with a half hourly frequency as far as Leeholme. A further two van-based minibuses were added in the form of two Renault-Dodge with bodywork by Northern Counties.

United immediately responded with their own 1D and 4D service, exactly copying Eden's 1C/4C and running just in front, and a similar tactic was put in place against the extra short 3C service to Leeholme. United placed regular drivers on the 1D and 4D and competition became quite intense,

especially between the staff of the two companies.

Eventually, with losses being made by both companies, United and Eden withdrew these competing services and there was some negotiations to introduce a settled network of services between Bishop Auckland, Shildon and Newton Aycliffe. Combined, the United 4/4A and Eden 91/92 provided a 15 minute frequency, but it was an uneasy truce.

Though Eden were still officially collaborating with Darlington Transport, the Dart name had fallen out of use and the relationship between the two companies became strained when DTC was put up for sale by their owners, Darlington Borough Council. Seeking to protect their service, Eden registered their own 91A route between the Horndale area of Newton Aycliffe and Darlington.

1992 also saw the sad passing of George Summerson, leaving Barry and David in charge of the company, ably assisted by John Godfrey, the traffic manager.

Another problem The Eden faced was the age of their fleet. Eden did explore the possibility of buying new buses, and a Dennis Dart demonstrator was used. The Dart was a lightweight, single-deck bus seating around 40, but did not impress. The last two Leyland Leopard service buses in the form of L12 and L14 were mainly confined to service 99. Durham County Council were also pushing for operators to have more accessible buses with lower entrance and exit steps and other features intended to be friendly towards the disabled and elderly. As a result, five second hand Leyland Nationals were sourced. The existing Leyland 510 engines the Nationals were fitted with, had a reputation for poor reliability and they were all replaced with Volvo engines and treated to a light refurbishment internally to bring them up to date. The Nationals were all given registration marks from Northern Ireland to further disguise their age.

On the back of this, Eden won a tender to operate service 217 from Ferryhill to Sunderland, and the 3C service was incorporated into it. The Leopard coaches were also fitted with brightly coloured handrails and step edging to comply with the contract specification.

Service 99 was by now suffering a terminal decline in ridership, the heavy industry along the route gone and the town of Spennymoor no longer a shopping destination. The two Renault-Dodge minibuses were allocated mainly to the

99 in an effort to cut costs, as they had superior fuel consumption as opposed to a Leopard or a National.

In 1994, Darlington Transport went into receivership, as a buyer could not be found for the business. Stagecoach was interested in buying DTC but they lost out on the bidding process. Unperturbed by this, they registered a network mirroring that of DTC, including the Darlington-Newton Aycliffe services and began running free buses about a month before their network was officially to begin (legally, they could not charge fares). Existing DTC drivers were offered cash and other incentives to join Stagecoach and many DTC employees took up the offer as they could see what was going to happen.

Stagecoach were undergoing a period of expansion at this point, especially in the North East by buying up the former municipal operators in the region. This left Durham as a potential hole in the Stagecoach North East network. North East Bus, who by now were the owners of United, were mindful of Stagecoach's aggressive tactics and with this in mind, again approached The Eden with a takeover bid. Faced with having to invest

heavily with newer buses, and still recovering from the costs incurred from operating competitively with United, the Summerson family agreed to sell to NEB in October 1995.

The Monopolies and Mergers Commission did not get involved in this instance, However, upon learning that United had taken over The Eden, some Eden staff left immediately. The operations were left at West Auckland for the time being, though United set about recasting the network with all the Eden operations to be transferred to United's Bishop Auckland depot.

The last day of Eden operation from West Auckland was the night of 31st December 1995, and Leyland Leopard L21 was the last bus in the garage driven by Steve Foster.

The Eden was retained as a trading unit under North East Bus. Only a few of the Eden buses remained in service, the Leopard coaches, remaining Metrorider and Sherpa were sold to dealers. The 165 and X65 services were merged into United's own Market Day special services to Stockton, but interestingly the 99 was retained initially, though operated with minibuses. This changed in 1997 when the 99 was withdrawn

N1 (YXI 3751) originated with Barrow Corporation. The seats were retrimmed in fresh moquette and had other features added to it such as highlighted step edges, designed to assist the visually impaired. The Volvo engines fitted to these buses gave them an interesting turn of speed! *(Steve Foster)*

832 (URB 822S) is so far the only double-deck vehicle to wear 'The Eden' fleetnames, albeit on United livery. It was designated for use on a scholars contract but often found its way onto local service work, and it is seen here in Shildon working service 91. *(Steve Foster)*

2471 (D471 EAJ), a Mercedes 608D minibus was transferred to the Eden company within North East Bus. It wears United livery but with basic 'Eden' fleetnames, and is about to set off to Ferryhill on service 217, which was originally Eden service 3C before the tender for the service from Ferryhill to Sunderland was gained. *(Ian Wilson)*

A curious picture of MAN 11.190/Optare Vecta 1514 wearing United fleet name but legally owned by Eden Bus Services, which had been retained by North East Bus as a separate operating company. *(Ian Wilson)*

1514 (K514 BHN) did eventually gain 'The Eden' fleetnames, as seen here loading passengers in Durham Bus Station. The Eden name and operating company was retained by North East Bus to compete for tendered work, with drivers on separate employment conditions and wages. The Eden 'unit' as it was termed did make a few tender gains, and took The Eden name to places not normally associated with the traditional company. *(Ian Wilson)*

Another view of 1514 (K514 BHN), a MAN 11.190/Optare Vecta seen this time in Ferryhill on service 217. The former Eden Leyland Nationals were transferred to the Teesside Motor Services division of North East Bus in the interests of depot type standardisation and two Optare Vectas were transferred into The Eden operating unit based at Bishop Auckland depot, which was used to tender for contracted work from Durham County Council. *(T Wightman)*

and replaced with service 7, running from Bishop Auckland to Tindale Crescent and picking up the old 99 route from there.

Reflecting the loss of industry, and also changing travel habits of employees at Aycliffe Trading Estate, the factory services from Leeholme and West Auckland were scaled back and eventually withdrawn. The Eden unit was used to tender for contracts from Durham County Council and the staff employed on the unit were on their own conditions, including a lower rate of pay. These lower costs enabled North East Bus to be more competitive when bidding for tenders. As an example, when Gardiners of Spennymoor signalled their intention to withdraw from local service work, North East Bus took the work on and placed it under the operation of The Eden.

It was intended that each NEB depot would have a low cost Eden unit, to take on contracted and tendered work, but in the end this did not extend further than Bishop Auckland depot.

Then came the unusual sight of buses in United livery, but with The Eden logos placed on them. These buses were officially owned by Eden Bus Services Limited, and any use on United services meant that 'on hire' notices had to be placed upon them, and vice-versa.

That was the situation until 1996, when North East Bus was bought out by the Cowie Group. Cowie then bought British Bus Holdings, and the whole operation was rebranded as Arriva, with United becoming Arriva Durham County. The Eden unit held on for a little while longer, but was extinct by 1999 when the company and name was laid dormant, with the corporate Arriva image being preferred.

This, however, is by no means the end of the story.....!

8 – THE EDEN RIDES AGAIN!

Graeme Scarlett was a driver for The Eden during the late 1970s/early 1980s. Having been brought up in Shildon, as a youngster he was familiar with the company and indeed caught The Eden bus to school, and knew a number of The Eden staff at that time, Margaret Torr being one who stands in his mind.

In 1999, he had begun his own bus company, trading as Grahams Motor Services, and began a town service in Shildon. The bus used was initially an Iveco Daily minibus painted in a livery not dissimilar to that of The Eden and occasionally used a conductress. The passengers remarked on what a "handy bus" it was, and the name Grahams Handy Bus was adopted.

Unfortunately, that service suffered intense competition from Arriva who did not take kindly to a small operator trying to muscle in on their patch and faced with running at a loss, the service was withdrawn. However, Graeme continued to operate school contracts for Durham County Council and in 2002, won a contract from Asda

Supermarkets to provide a free service from the Bishop Auckland bus station to their new store that was built on the site of the former Wilsons Forge, in Bishop Auckland, and the bus carried an overall livery for Asda.

Initially, the bus ran as being operated by Grahams Handy Bus, but behind the scenes, Graeme was in advanced negotiations to buy the intellectual property rights for The Eden from Arriva. After some deep negotiation, Arriva agreed to sell the rights to use The Eden name to Graeme.

Thus, in 2004, the familiar The Eden name and livery returned on another Mercedes 709 minibus, and following The Eden traditional fleet numbering scheme, the two Mercedes received fleet numbers M2 and M3. A short town service in Bishop Auckland was also won on tender from Durham County Council, running from the Bus Station to Etherley Lane via Princes Street. This was done between trips on the Asda shuttle.

2005 saw the return of service 99, running between West Auckland and Shildon, and M3 was put to use on it. Sadly, passenger numbers were poor and the service had to be de-registered.

The first bus to carry 'The Eden' name under the ownership of Graeme Scarlett was F444 GAT, a Mercedes 709 minibus which gained the fleet number of M2. It carried an overall advert for the Asda supermarket in Bishop Auckland and The Eden gained the contract to operate the free shoppers service from the bus station to the new store when it opened. *(John Carter)*

M3 (L634 VCV) was the first bus to carry full 'The Eden' livery since the name and livery was retired by Arriva. M3 was used as a reserve vehicle on the Asda service and caused quite a stir the first time it appeared on the streets! *(John Carter)*

OS1 (MX57 URA) was an Optare Solo acquired to operate service 83 from Cockfield to Woodland which was won on tender in 2008, and the first brand new bus to carry Eden livery since the trio of MCW Metroriders twenty years earlier. *(S Gray)*

At the time of writing, The Eden operate the tender for service 17, a local service in Newton Aycliffe, and continues the association with the town and The Eden who pioneered the first bus service in the then new town. OS6 (YE52 FHP) is the usual bus allocated to the 17. *(Matthew Jimmison)*

D1 (V732 DNL) is a Dennis Dart SLF with Plaxton 'Mini Pointer Dart' bodywork, acquired from Go North East. Initially used on the 83 service from Cockfield to Woodland, D1 is seen here in Bishop Auckland Bus Station on the Asda Free Bus service. *(Matthew Williamson)*

P1 (MX06 AEA) is an unusual Plaxton Primo midibus, seen here at West Auckland village centre. The Primo was based on the chassis of the Enterprise Plasma which was made in Hungary. It does, however, look quite resplendent in The Eden livery! *(S Gray)*

OS7 (YG02 FVU) is an Optare Solo acquired from Blackpool Transport in 2015. The location here is Shildon town centre, and OS7 is working a special service on behalf of Locomotion – The National Railway Museum which is located on the outskirts of Shildon. Graeme Scarlett is the driver here. *(S Gray)*

In 2008, the tender for service 83 was won from Durham County Council. This had its origins in a former OK service from Cockfield to Woodland. A new Optare Solo was obtained to operate the service, becoming OS1 (MX57 URA).

In 2011, Graeme secured the lease of the original Summerson's garage in West Auckland. It had been sold to a local entrepreneur who leased it to a storage company, but it had subsequently become vacant for a few years. Some work was required to refurbish the building and grounds, and in early 2012, The Eden returned to its most familiar operating centre. A further contract to operate a free shuttle bus between Bishop Auckland bus station and the new Tesco supermarket at Tindale Crescent was also successfully obtained.

2013 saw the loss of the service 83 contract to Scarlet Band in the tendering round of that year, but, fittingly, in 2014 a tender was won from Durham County Council to operate the Newton Aycliffe Town Service, over 60 years since the Summersons developed the first bus services in Newton Aycliffe. This town service is a very similar operation to that also operated by The Eden in the early 1990s.

In between all of this, Graeme also secured a former Summerson's bus, a Leyland Leopard with Plaxton Derwent bodywork in the form of L14 (PPT 446P), which required major restoration work. Much of the work was carried out by Kenny Nesbitt, who practically rebuilt the body, but sadly, Kenny died before the work was complete, nevertheless in 2013, L14 returned to the road with its first MOT pass in over 15 years. She is exhibited at local bus rallies where she always gets much attention from the public, and your author had the honour of driving her at a friend's wedding in 2015. The Eden fleet today mainly consists of Optare Solos, smartly turned out in The Eden livery.

There is a small but growing team of dedicated staff, who strive to maintain the high standards set by both the Summerson family and Graeme Scarlett over the last 90 years, and for which The Eden name is famed in Bishop Auckland, Shildon and the surrounding areas.

The bus industry has been through many changes over that time, but the familiar The Eden name and livery remain with us, and hopefully will be for many years to come.

This photos was taken by David Summerson at a company staff Christmas function in the 1970s. These were an annual event and held to thank the staff for their efforts throughout the year, usually held at the Sun Inn at Wackerfield. *(Summerson Family Collection)*